ALSO BY

MASSIMO RECALCATI

The Night in Gethsemane

CAIN'S ACT

Massimo Recalcati

CAIN'S ACT

*Translated from the Italian
by Will Schutt*

Europa
editions

Europa Editions
27 Union Square West, Suite 302
New York, NY 10003
www.europaeditions.com
info@europaeditions.com

Translation by Will Schutt
Original title: *Il gesto di Caino*
Translation copyright © 2022 by Europa Editions

Library of Congress Cataloging in Publication Data is available
ISBN 978-1-60945-815-7

Recalcati, Massimo
Cain's Act

Art direction by Emanuele Ragnisco
instagram.com/emanueleragnisco

Cover image: *Cain kills Abel*, Ghent Altarpiece.
© akg-images/Mondadori Portfolio.

Prepress by Grafica Punto Print – Rome

Printed in the USA

CONTENTS

While they were in the field,
Cain attacked his brother Abel and killed him.
—GENESIS 4:8

CAIN'S ACT

INTRODUCTION

Cain's act is merciless. He kills his brother and stains the earth with Abel's blood. His act leaves no hope, permits no dialogue, and fails to stop heinous, hate-fueled violence. With this act, the story of humankind begins. We know that love of thy neighbor is the final and most fundamental word arrived at by biblical logos. But it is not the first word. It comes after Cain's act.

Can we assume that loving thy neighbor is a response to this awful act? Can we assume that loving thy neighbor can only be achieved by way of Cain's destructive act? What is certain is that in the biblical narrative loving thy neighbor occurs after the original experience of hatred. The narrative espouses no altruism whatsoever. It does not describe a "humanistic" pastoral without shadows. It does not support the myth of humans as born "good" or conceal the fact that they have harbored the temptations of hatred and destruction far longer than the temptations of love.

The biblical story appears implacable and clear-eyed: criminal violence is introduced into the world by man alone and forever marks his relationship to his brother. Nature's innocence seems shaken by this unexpected, tumultuous event, an event that is not the result of a rash impulse, much less a regression to a primitive animal state. It involves a rupture between man and nature and between man and his fellow man—a rupture which defines him. To be more exact, the Bible shows how violence makes manifest the perverse and narcissistic character of human desire: our drive to destroy alterity, our aspiration to become divine, our desire to be God.[1] Lurking beneath this drive is real human ambition and the ultimate origin of our temptation to commit violence. This theme runs through the entire narrative of the Bible. True sin does not—as Augustine classically argued—privilege the created at the expense of the Creator, inverting the ontological order; true sin leads the created to equate itself with the Creator and compels man to want to be like God. Human desire is in fact deluded into thinking that there can be a being that does not know the negative, lacerating experience of lack. The symbolic existence of the Law of the Word shapes up to be an unfair interference that compromises and inevitably postpones the making of this being. That is why hatred is chiefly directed at language. Indeed, the Law of the Word makes it impossible to exist without the Other—and therefore without lack. Hence man's hatred for this Law that forces him to recognize the insurmountable character of his own "lack of being," which, as Lacan notes, is not only a lack of something but a lack that pervades human subjectivity itself. The true objective of hatred is the lack—generated by the Law of the Word—that tethers the subject to the Other.

To commit violence is to try to wriggle out of this tether and achieve our goal of destroying the inescapable mediation of the Other. The perverse object of human desire is to fashion oneself into a self-sufficient being, an *ens causa sui*, a master of one's own making. As with violence, so with hallucination: we are under the illusion that such a goal can be achieved via "a shortcut," as Freud would say, by bypassing the difficult and unavoidable mediation of the Other. If the action of loving thy neighbor accepts the otherness of the Other without seeking correspondence or reciprocity, and causes man to recognize his dependence on the existence of the Other, then hatred drives him to destroy the Other as the seat of his alienation in the name of an absolute ideal of autonomy and independence, in the name of making himself into a being without lack.

Cain's fratricidal act makes a dramatic and traumatic entrance at the very start of the Bible. It is the second major transgression, the first being Adam and Eve's theft of the apple from the tree of knowledge of good and evil. The negative energy of man is strikingly present from the beginning; the drive to break the Law does not define man's behavior or psychological attitude so much as it defines his will to elevate himself—above and beyond the symbolic Law of the Word—into a totality, rejecting the lack that is his lot. The serpent promises Eve this very thing in Genesis: eat the forbidden fruit, violate the Law, and you shall become divine and erase the insurmountable lack that, as I've said, defines man.

Like his parents, Cain is forced to face the trauma of the impossible. His life as an only son is traumatically intruded on by Abel; the narcissism of his Ego butts up against the judgment of God, who prefers the offerings of Cain's younger brother to Cain's own. It is all too much for him. In his homicidal fury, he means to strike the person who caused his fall. Abel is not perceived as a brother and deserving of love but as deserving of hatred, because he is responsible for robbing Cain of the narcissistic prestige Cain enjoys with his mother and with God.

But we mustn't read the fratricidal act as merely a perverse deviation from the path of love; our propensity for fratricide is what defines us as human beings. *Harming thy neighbor comes before loving thy neighbor.* If my neighbor reveals my internal limitation, and therefore an otherness that is not simply external but also internal, because my existence cannot exist without the Other, then hatred seeks to destroy this same alterity and establish the subject as absolute and independent. That is why, as Saint Ambrose was one of the first to observe, Cain and Abel are not only two autonomous literary figures in the Bible—two characters—but two "internal" parts of the subject, emblems of a division that exists in each of us. Rather than endorse a moralist reading of the brothers' conflict—Cain the evil versus Abel the good—which would suggest that there is a clear divide between good and evil, we must understand the complexity of Cain's journey as a movement of progressive subjectivation of that divide: he commits a brutal act, then refuses to take responsibility for it, then embarks upon life in the city. If the murderer's violence stands in opposition to the Law of the Word—"violence," says Deleuze, "does not speak"[2]—Cain, a bit like Sophocles' Oedipus, goes from being wracked with guilt to cursing God, from wandering the earth performing hard labor to building the first human city to becoming at last a father. It is a slow and difficult process conditioned, for starters, by God's having protected Cain with a "mark." By doing so, God breaks the chain of violence that would have the murder murdered and frees the Law from the logic of retaliation and vengeance, allowing Cain to mourn his actions without worrying about whether he might be killed. Thus, the mark that God puts on Cain's forehead is both a mark of grief for the death of his brother and a mark of protection against an exclusively punitive Law that would kill anyone who has killed. The sign of God, which contradicts this version of the Law, divorces Cain from his action and reminds us that just because he is guilty of murder doesn't authorize us to identify him as just a "murderer."

Freud, who was Jewish, conceives of the history of humanity as the history of a never-ending and heinous series of murders, and our subconscious as having an aptitude for criminal behavior. Our task is the same, therefore, as the one that Cain had to take up the day after his desperate and pitiless act: to transform the lawless violence of hatred—an expression of narcissism on the part of the One to erase the lack that binds him to the Other—into a new bond with the Other; to allow the Law of the Word to break the endless cycle of hatred and destruction.

M.R.
April 2020, Milan

It is true that those who like fairy stories turn
a deaf ear to talk of man's innate tendencies to "evil,"
aggression, destruction, and thus also to cruelty.
—SIGMUND FREUD,
Civilization and Its Discontents (1929)

In the Beginning Was Cain

I n the Bible, the first act of the son is to murder his own brother in cold blood. With no remorse, with no pity. Violence comes naturally to man, it seems. We are as profoundly implicated by Cain's fate as we are by that of Sophocles' Oedipus (as read by Freud). Both sons are "cursed," swept up in the vortex of violence and the drama of guilt. Both kill their own blood, their closest neighbor, their next of kin. The Bible places Cain's story at the origin of all human descendants. His act belongs to the primeval history of humankind. Freud puts it plainly:

> The primeval history of mankind is filled with murder. Even today the history of the world which our children learn at school is essentially a long series of murders of peoples.[3]

The primeval event that inaugurates the history of all humankind is, therefore, fratricide: the brother not loved but killed. That trauma is a legacy of the human world, not the animal world. In fact, there is no such thing as crime in the animal world, for violent instincts are linked to an organism's natural needs (whether it is defending itself or on the attack). Human life, on the other hand, involves the temptation—"human, all too human"—to do violence. What temptation? The temptation to extinguish the separated life of the Other, to deny the Other's alterity. Killing means suppressing the alterity of the Other, which we view as an intolerable check on our freedom. For this reason, Freud, closely adhering to the biblical narrative, does not hesitate to suggest that murder lies at the origin of the human species. The father of psychoanalysis accepts the biblical idea that mankind has forever been disgraced by Cain's act:

> Men are not gentle, friendly creatures wishing for love, who simply defend themselves if they are attacked, but that a powerful measure of desire for aggression has to be reckoned as part of their instinctual endowment.[4]

Biblical logos—like its psychoanalytical counterpart—does not tiptoe around human violence; on the contrary, violence becomes one of its most important and frequently recurring subjects. It is no accident that the story of humankind opens with Cain murdering Abel. Not with love, trust, solidarity, or acceptance of the Other, but with the destruction and brutal murder of the Other. To place Cain's act at the beginning is to bring into relief—rather than conceal—cruelty, horror of the negative, and aggression as primary human impulses. Each of us possesses the urge to kill, to put down our rival, to leave our mark on the world. *Homo homini lupus*, as Hobbes has it, and Freud will pick up the theme in *Civilization and Its Discontents*. In terms of the unconscious, we have all been, and all are, Cain. For Freud, this is the structurally criminal aspect of the unconscious. "If we are to be judged by our unconscious wishful impulses," he writes, "we ourselves are, like primaeval men, a gang of murderers."[5]

Violence, unlike animal instinct and understood as a

destructive impulse, defines human life—and no other forms of life. If in animals violence springs from the same set of instincts as the urge to reproduce, in humans it appears chiefly motivated by the temptation to get out from under the burdensome presence of the alterity of the Other.

CREATION

In Creation, the biblical God miraculously begets the world out of nothing (*ex nihilo*), breathing life into an endless variety of beings who will inhabit it. Divine creation affirms the splendor of diversity. Levinas explains that it is not a degradation-emanation of the world coming into being out of the being of God, as Neoplatonic theory would have it, not the world as an expression that issues from God, but an unprecedented excess wherein all creatures are free to be their unique selves: the birds in the sky, the fish in the sea, humans on earth. Creation is a multiplicity that exceeds any notion of totality:

> [T]he idea of creation *ex nihilo* expresses a multiplicity not united into a totality; the creature is an existence which indeed does depend on an Other, but not as a part that is separated from it. Creation *ex nihilo* breaks with system, posits a being outside of every system, that is, there where its freedom is possible . . . What is essential to created existence is its separation with regard to the Infinite.[6]

On the one hand, the creature emerges in the world from the creationary act of God. On the other, its existence is separate from God—unique, singular, unrepeatable. Its multiplicity cannot be traced back to a "system" or "totality." This is exactly what gives creation its splendor: each creature depends on the act of creation, yet the act of creation renders it utterly free, a thing unto itself, unique, absolute. The separation of creature from Creator grants the creature its independent stature, even if the creature still owes its original existence to the Creator.[7] The entire created universe is animated by this generative diversity that not only draws distinctions between animals but divides human beings into male and female.

In the Bible, God's power does not stop at his extraordinary ability to set creation in motion. More importantly, he has the power to bring things into existence by the force of language, by giving things a name. Only by being named do the things of the world acquire a singular, distinguishing identity. To give a thing a name is to set it apart, to differentiate it, to distinguish it. In this sense, the Law of language prolongs God's act of creation. A name gives life to the Thing and saves it from indistinction and indeterminacy. This fundamental nexus seals the bond between God and the word, a bond that is, famously, one of the great themes of the Bible. A name does not simply designate a "thing" by naming it, but, naming it, gives it existence, ushers it onto the world's stage, separates it from nothingness. As young Hegel would put it, the divine word annihilates the immediacy of Nature and places nature in the realm of the Spirit.[8] God's names render the dark "night" and the light "day," the gathering together of waters "seas" and dry land "Earth" (Gen. 1:1-9), transforming undifferentiated chaos into the differentiated phenomena of the world. It is the word that shapes being, retrieving it from the shadowy abyss of the Origin. It is the word that illuminates all things, the first Law that makes possible the separate and unique form of every creature. "God said . . . And it was so" (Gen. 1:1-31) is repeated throughout the process of creation *ex nihilo*.

BREAKING THE LAW

After Creation, the Bible tells the story of two major transgressions. The first involves Adam and Eve and takes place in the Garden of Eden, when they steal the fruit from the tree of knowledge of good and evil.

The story is well known: God commands Adam and Eve not to taste of the fruit, and that command incites them to break the Law. To the same degree that the Law forbids humans to access the tree of knowledge, it also inflames, at the same time, their human desire to violate that rule. It is the birth of the Law—God's command—that rouses them to break the Law. Paul the Apostle makes this clear when he argues, in a formulation often cited by Lacan, that it is only because of the Law that the experience of sin exists (Rom. 3:1-20). Meaning the drawing of boundaries—the symbolic act of the Law—kindles our desire to transgress them. This explains why crime does not entail the dehumanization of people but instead reveals people at their most profoundly human. Only a being who grasps the meaning of the Law can commit crimes; only humans fail to adhere unwaveringly to naked life, to the immediacy of vital instinct. Whereas animal life is wholly governed by biological programming, human life is laid bare by the very existence of the Law. It is in the lives of humans that the power of the Law is evident, not in the lives of ants, lions, beavers, or dogs. Those forms of existence correspond entirely and exclusively to the laws of instinct. Unlike animals, adrift in the immediate present, humans aspire to a consciousness that goes beyond the immediacy of nature. Humans want to know the meaning of life.

In fact, the self-reflexive drive defines human life as duplicate, capable of self-differentiation, as opposed to animal life, which fully coincides with its own existence. While an animal's life is one of immersion in, and identity with, the vital process, a human life never coincides with such a process because of its inborn negativity: human life is its existence but never fully coincides with it. Life is only made human through the meaning of the Law, which distorts a life of instinct. Indeed, stealing is not instinctive, because stealing cannot be defined as a crime unless there is the symbolic existence of the Law that forbids theft. It is no accident that the Bible begins with the story of two key human crimes: theft and murder. The Law does not emerge in response to crime; the Law establishes crime as a distinct possibility for humans. The propensity to break the law is not only a possibility but a fundamental inclination of human life.

Becoming God:
The Promise of the Jealous Serpent

When Adam and Eve are forbidden from eating from the tree of knowledge of good and evil, the Law becomes a check on knowledge. Humans cannot know what God knows, i.e., *they cannot know everything.* Faced with this limitation (which, read the right way, allows for the possibility of attaining knowledge, since by definition knowing becomes possible the moment one is precluded from knowing all there is to know) man is driven not only by *a desire to know what God knows* but by *a desire to be like God.* The subject that it raises—envy—will be crucial to the story of Cain. But envy poisons Adam and Eve first, filling them with an ardor to have what doesn't belong to them and which seems to reject all limitations whatsoever.

In the Bible it is the serpent that infects them with envy and drives them to break the Law. With what arguments does he do it? Firstly, he insinuates that God wants to hoard the spoils of Creation for himself, that he intends to keep his creatures from living life to the fullest so that he can wield his own unchecked power over them. The serpent portrays God as a selfish master, incapable of thinking of the well-being of others. He maliciously suggests that the only reason for God's divine command is to "guarantee God's sovereignty over the life of man."[9] His venomous insinuations seek to slander God, to knock God off his pedestal by showing them his insane face, unquenchable cupidity, and brute tyranny. The serpent craftily plants the seed of doubt: "Did God really say: 'You must not eat from any tree in the garden?'" (Gen. 3:1) The same question will be dramatically echoed in the Book of Job. How could God do such a thing?

The serpent paints a picture of a titanic, severe, egotistical Father who wants to enjoy his creation with impunity while for no good reason prohibiting his children from doing the same.[10] Many neurotics are haunted by this phantom of a father whose authority masks a secret and perverse jouissance, who pretends to represent the Law while hidden between the lines of the Law is lawless jouissance. This is a distorted version of the father who applies the law merely to safeguard the exceptional joy he takes in being above the law. The serpent's insinuations seek to degrade, de-idealize, discredit, and pervert the image of God. Such is the task of all "serpents": to defame, to foment hatred, to discredit. Yet in her initial reply Eve correctly points out that God has only prohibited them from eating from one tree, the tree of knowledge:

> The woman said to the serpent, "We may eat fruit from the trees in the garden, but God did say, 'You must not eat fruit from the tree that is in the middle of the garden, and you must not touch it, or you will die.'" (Gen 3:2-3)

But her objection to the serpent's hisses is not enough to prevent her from becoming jealous. What the serpent does not want to acknowledge is that pleasure is by no means impeded by the Law, for it is only thanks to the

Law—to the splendor of God's creation—that one can eat fruit from trees in the first place. Only the tree of knowledge, where the true meaning of good and evil is safeguarded, is off-limits. God bars man from knowing good and evil, from knowing absolute truth, from knowing what God knows, from knowing everything, because he made him "man," and, as such, not self-sufficient, incapable of self-generating, excluded from an absolute condition of fullness. Yet God is not a sadistic father who takes pleasure in his omnipotence, who applies the Law at whim, but a father who intends to imbue the Law with human—earthly—meaning and preserve the experience of impossibility: we cannot know everything, take pleasure in everything, have everything, be everything. The serpent's plan—his profound temptation—is, on the other hand, to attain the fullness of God, to achieve a condition of life that does not include lack, that actually turns man into a God (Gen. 3:5). But the serpent overlooks the fact that when enjoyment, jouissance, is separated from the Law, when it conflicts with the Law, it becomes, as the following verses remind us, an enjoyment that leads to death:

> You are free to eat from any tree in the garden; but you must not eat from the tree of the knowledge of good and evil, for when you eat from it you will certainly die. (Gen. 2: 16-17)

No accident, then, that Lacan associates the figure of "deadly enjoyment" with an incestuous, regressive, ruinous enjoyment in life that rejects the Law of castration, the Law that inscribes in humans the sense of the impossible.[11] Thus it is important to highlight the relationship, established by the word of God, between the Law and death. Not simply the Law as repressive and deadly, the Law which vows to put to death anyone who breaks it, but the deadly enjoyment that engulfs those who carry in their heart the meaning of the Law, the knowledge that reality presents us with impossibilities: it is impossible to be, to have, to know, to enjoy everything.

The serpent's act is motivated by pure envy. It seeks to unmask the Other, to reveal the Other not as the site of the Law that makes humans human but as a site of tyrannical enjoyment that arbitrarily robs life of enjoyment. The ghost of the joy-seeking father in our subconscious is here in full force. The serpent sows discord and doubt, it strives to pervert the gaze of Adam and Eve, to cloud the evidence of God's love and the generosity of his Creation, to make them forget that God created humans in his own image. Sequeri describes it perfectly:

> Maybe the serpent is right. Our submission to God depends on our ignorance, our inexperience, and the gullibility with which we accept pre-established distinctions between good and evil. Maybe not everything forbidden us is malignant [. . .] If God is as the serpent suggests, the threat of death he poses to man becomes radical and insurmountable. Therefore, any appreciation of goodness, any allure of beauty, and any increase in knowledge is dangerous.[12]

The serpent foments, defames, and slanders. It offers a mendacious image of the Law and nurtures a childish idea of freedom that views the impossible as the result of a mere arbitrary act, as if by forbidding them from the tree of knowledge God were selfishly guarding his prestige and interests, keeping man in a passive, infantile state of submission. As if he were keeping the knowledge of good and evil for himself and leaving man ignorant. As if he were enjoying his omnipotence and consigning men to helpless innocence. For Adam, Eve, and the snake, the mention of death ("for when you eat from it you will certainly die") does not confirm that there are limits inscribed in the human heart; it proves that God is abusing his authority. The serpent venomously misrepresents the impossible as nothing more than God's hostile—domineering—will toward humans. But didn't God grant Adam and Eve their rare place in Creation? Weren't they made "in his own image"? Is not the very existence of the world unmistakable proof of God's love of man? The jealous, cunning snake tries to obscure this evidence and turn love into hate. We are bearing witness to what psychoanalysts call negative transference. Love for the Other gives way to permanent revendication, fueled purely by envy: constant criticism, continual accusations, a refusal to relate, de-supposition of knowledge. None of the signs and actions of the Other reflect his lovability but instead seem to reveal him as patently untrustworthy and devious. The ideal, loving father is replaced by the power-hungry, joy-seeking father/master; amorous idealization by resentful aggression.

The serpent tries to make humans transfer negative feelings onto God; the Law ceases to serve man and is revealed to be merely an arbitrary power that forces man to serve its own masochistic ends. The serpent appeals to unlimited freedom propped up by an illusory promise that, once deified, man shall inherit God's powers. In the Bible the serpent's words are as clear as day: "[Y]our eyes will be opened, and you will be like God, knowing good and evil" (Gen. 3:4). You won't need him anymore! You'll be omnipotent! He tempts them with assurances that they will become godlike, attain God's plenitude, not have to content themselves with human life. The temptation is to put God and man, father and son, on equal footing; it promises to deify man in an exchange that excludes difference. It is a *perverse promise,* for it seeks to rid the human experience of impossibility, consequently stripping the law of its human meaning, and most of all annul the ontological difference that separates the Creator from the creature, God from man. This temptation qualifies deadly enjoyment: to achieve a form of enjoyment that excludes separation, an absolute enjoyment, free of lack, capable of eliminating difference, and closing the gap between man and God. This same illusion inspires all libertarian teachings that claim the Other serves no purpose, that the Other is just a hindrance, that growth is self-generated, that the Law is an obstacle to exercising one's freedom to the fullest.

The end result of the serpent's calumny and totalitarian temptation conceals the destructive side of deadly enjoyment. Indeed, the serpent symbolizes an obtuse, libertarian understanding of the Law as a drag on freedom, a pointless obstacle to the full development of life. The Bible constantly begs the question: What is the ultimate meaning of the Law? Is God, qua symbol of the Law, master of the Law? Does God enjoy the Law that he himself symbolizes with impunity? Or, as Jesus described the dilemma, is the Law made for man or man for the Law?

Nakedness Exposed

T he first mythical transgression ends with a fall; the deadly enjoyment that promised to make Adam and Eve divine winds up ruining human life itself. The mirage of totalization dissolves, and Adam and Eve find themselves lost, bewildered by existence. For the first time they can see that they are naked, a sign of their break with Nature, their laceration, their separation from the natural flow of life that other living creatures exist in. Humans are, in fact, the only animals to see themselves as naked. Other animals cannot conceive of nakedness because, paradoxically, they are always naked; they have no sense of modesty or shame. To them, nakedness is a natural condition. Always naked, the animal body is never truly naked. If nakedness is achieved only after being undressed, being stripped, if nakedness implies that a veil has fallen, then the animal body can never apprehend the deeper meaning of nakedness. Adam and Eve's discovery of the naked body on the contrary radically subverts their temptation, inflamed by the serpent, to be omnipotent and godlike, and reveals them to be human. This nakedness symbolizes how far they have fallen, how helpless they are, after breaking the law.

This nakedness is not, however, the same as Adam and Eve's original nakedness at the time of Creation. There was no shame attached to that first form of nakedness (Gen. 2:25) because there was no guilty perception of nakedness; it was a nakedness without shame and confusion—just as nakedness is for all other animals—identified with the vitality of the body, with belonging to nature. This *second nakedness* can only appear in the context of the traumatic break from the *first nakedness*, which is connected to man's identification with his natural life. This second nakedness is an unveiled display of the body that causes shame; that reveals to humans their vulnerability; that, indeed, strips them of the illusion that they are deities. It is a nakedness that, arousing feelings of guilt and shame, must be covered, cloaked, concealed. It occurs right after they take the first bite of the forbidden fruit: "Then the eyes of both were opened, and they knew that they were naked" (Gen. 3:7). This undressing radically demonstrates how the perverse spell, which would put humans on an equal footing with God, is broken. For the first time, humans sense just how naked, how powerless, and how cut off from the animal world they really are.

GOD'S LAW

The fear of God appears for the first time in the history of humankind as God gazes upon the naked bodies of Adam and Eve and the two await the death promised by God's Law. Their nakedness betrays their overwhelming sense of guilt as they expect to be punished for the sin they have committed. But contrary to what the hateful, jealous serpent had insinuated, it isn't God's wish to sentence them to death. Quite the opposite. The Law is never on the side of death; it is always on the side of life. It is no accident that when the Law is first applied, the lives of Adam and Eve are spared, further contradicting the serpent. No retribution, no death sentence, no execution. It is a fundamental passage that encapsulates the character of God in the Bible: divine Law is not applied with sadistic pleasure, its aim is not to punish, it is neither punitive nor menacing. Nor is the biblical God a cruel, merciless, vindictive deity. Here we have another instance of a god who would rather go back on his word than give the impression that the Law is violent. He delays applying the Law that he himself had promulgated (if "you eat it . . . you will die"), commuting the transgressors' death sentence. If that weren't enough, moved to pity, he clothes Adam and Eve with "garments of skin" (Gen. 3:21), an act of pity that none but a god who has the interest of his creatures at heart would perform. Therefore he is not an omnipotent God who flexes his might but a God whose profoundly loving gesture is, if anything, maternal. He restores dignity to those who have broken the Law. Only the serpent is forever cursed, while man is left to brave the path of history and endure the pain of existence, separation, and the irreversible loss of innocence. Man did not err by passively submitting to God's will—as the malicious jealous serpent has it—but by mistaking his "resemblance" to God—a resemblance desired by the Creator himself—as a sign that man and God were equals and perfectly mirrored each other. Man's error, insufflated by the serpent, was to *want to be like God*, to want to breach the real limit of impossibility. The error was to choose deadly enjoyment and reject the meaning of the Law.

THE SECOND TRANSGRESSION:
VIOLENCE AND ENVY

The second major human transgression of the Law centers not on stealing the fruit of the tree of knowledge but on murdering one's brother. Its protagonists are not Adam, Eve, and the serpent but the dramatic figures of Cain and his brother Abel. And what it teaches us is radical: violence at its most heinous involves not strangers but brothers. This narrative choice means to demonstrate how, if we are really to confront the grim phenomenon of human violence, we must assume that each of us harbors an inner Cain, that human violence cannot be put down to defensive or aggressive instinct (as it can in the animal world) but instead lies at the heart of our most intimate bonds. It is Saint Ambrose who, Freud-like, invites us to consider Cain and Abel as "inner parts" of the subject, emblems of the subject's internal quarrel and ethical divide, of a clash between good and evil where one side will prevail over the other.[13]

My brother is my own flesh and blood, part of my very being. So Cain and Abel embody a deadly discord that exists within us—not without. That is why the Bible places the drama of fratricide at the start of its narrative. The violence it portrays is far more radical than basic instinct (defensive or aggressive). Cain does not lash out at a stranger, nemesis, or usurper, but at the person closest to him, his next of kin. It is an attack on our brother, our own blood, offspring of our parents, the person with whom we share the same provenance. Cain teaches us that violence is not the result of human regression to an animal state; violence does not erupt because man turns into a beast. In fact, the temptation to commit violence doesn't exist in the animal world, because in that world violence is connected not to desire and its unconscious ghosts but to the pure law of instinct. For that matter, neither is there such a thing as crime (or madness) in the animal world.

By situating transgression and violence at the start of the narrative, immediately after Creation, the Bible reaffirms the anthropological axiom that *man alone introduces crime into history*. This is the original character that biblical logos attributes to Cain's act: the first thing man does outside of Eden is commit fratricide. He expresses neither love for his neighbor nor gratitude to God or Creation, neither solidarity nor brotherhood, neither friendship nor love. As we have already seen, the Bible makes no concessions. It does not provide a rhetorical or idealized depiction of man. It does not shy from arguing that humans have a penchant for violence. Freud, too, affirmed this, in his way: at the origin of life, there is no integrative capacity of love; there is, however, the expulsive violence of hatred.[14] Meaning that human beings are not, as Aristotle's theory of man as a "social animal" has it, simply open to the world—they do not live to love their neighbor—because world and neighbor are primarily regarded as threatening, hostile intrusions on the life of the subject. Abel is for Cain primarily an intrusion. The existence of the second born cannot help but feel like a blow to the firstborn's joy and his phallic prestige in his mother's eyes.

We shall come back to this. For the moment we need simply define this penchant for hate-fueled violence as a primary human drive. And add that human violence is not
merely a measure of self-defense or protection; above all
else, it is, apparently, something we actually desire.
Whereas thought develops out of our recognition that we
cannot control the disquietude of life, violence holds out
the promise of getting what we want in one fell swoop. It
occurs between individuals the same as between nations or
ethnic groups. Violence fools us into thinking that we can
obtain what we desire and skip over the long obligatory
route of symbolic mediation established by the Law of the
word; that we do not have to wait to be gratified. Yet original violence is not blind. It is not an expression of unre-
strained urges or animal reflex. Before murdering Abel,
Cain displays an intense hatred for and envy of his brother,
a hatred that never ebbs but continues to feed itself. Is that
not enough of an outrage to the principles of common
sense and goodwill? Shouldn't the bond between siblings
be void of hatred? Shouldn't that bond be built on solidarity and love, the paradigm of positive relations?

Anticipating Freud, the Bible shows that the destructive drive is one of the unconscious's main predispositions
and precedes loving devotion. We saw this earlier, in the
evil figure of the serpent who instigates the first transgression. In fact, it is the serpent, not Cain, who darkens
Creation with envy. Like the serpent, Cain sees God's
actions as arbitrarily motivated. Like the serpent, Cain is
haunted by the neurotic ghost of a father/master, a perverse father who crushes the life of his children and
applies the Law at whim. And, as was the case with his
parents before him, inflamed by the serpent, Cain, as we

shall further see, flouts the Law of the father and questions his symbolic authority. This is the rebellious, romantic, anarchical side of Cain championed by many readers. José Saramago, for one, describes Cain as working to destroy the creation of an unjust and jealous God in order to free humankind. More recently, Andrea Camilleri extolled Cain as a Promethean figure, a builder of cities and culture.[15]

In humanity's second major transgression, the brother killer appears clearly blinded by jealousy. Cain is a dramatic figure not because he challenges God, Prometheus-like, but because he is held hostage to his own envious fantasies. His crime is not a heroic revolt against God's despotic arbitrariness; it demonstrates how jealousy is intimately wedded to the death drive. It is no accident that, where there is envy, there is no positive affirmation of joie de vivre, only "sorrow at another's good," as Thomas Aquinas famously has it. Then why does jealousy exert such a strong hold on human beings? How can it sweep away life with death?

Whatever qualities or possessions the envied may have are never the cause of envy. What we really envy is the life of the Other: the plenitude, wealth, and otherness of the Other's life. Hence Lacan can assert that the true object of envy is life itself; that envy is always, at root, envy of life.[16]

Cain's murderous act is shrouded in mystery. We are in the habit of thinking of violence as a form of recourse taken against our enemies, as arising from our original tendency to mistake, as Freud puts it, "the alien for the hostile."[17] In this sense, hatred, as has been said, precedes love, because hatred is man's first reaction to the Other, who disturbs or threatens the fixed boundaries of man's identity. But the story of Cain would appear to complicate this idea. As we have seen, Cain attacks not a stranger but his own kin, not a foreigner but his closest neighbor. His violence is not directed at an invader or sworn enemy but at his brother. It ranks among the most difficult, vexing points of the biblical story. Cain (the murderer) shares the same blood as Abel (the murdered), thereby forcing us to give the foreigner another face. The foreigner does not come from distant lands or live across the border from us; the foreigner resides under the same roof. It is a foreigner within, not without.

Why does Cain strike his brother dead? As the text of the Bible has it, Cain could not stand the preferential treatment that God showed Abel. We should immediately note that this frustration that Cain finds so intolerable reveals something about his character: *He cannot tolerate not being the only one.* In this sense, his action reveals that envy and narcissism lie at the root of human violence. Jealous hatred is an all-consuming passion because it seeks to impress upon the whole world the glorious narcissistic image of the "I." Cain, like his parents, appears to have been bitten by the serpent of envy. The violence he unleashes on his neighbor and not on an outsider, on his brother and not his enemy, bears the indelible mark of envy, since generally speaking the target of envy is never an unknown entity, but that which we would like to be and fail at being, our unattainable ideal, the person who embodies the narcissistic image we have of ourselves. In fact, the object of our envy is always those who are like us yet either have more than we have or are more than we are. We envy those who are like us, not different from us. In other words, the target of envy embodies the envier's secret ideal of him or herself. And it is this same jealous hatred that places the weapon in Cain's hand.

That said, for Eve, Abel, whose name means, incidentally, "smoke, steam, vanity,"[18] i.e., something flimsy and valueless, is not the ideal son. In her eyes, Cain is the ideal son, as far as he is her exclusive property. Eve's affection is not, therefore, the source of Cain's jealousy.

THE INTRUDER: CAIN AND NARCISSUS

L ife does not, then, begin with fraternal feeling but with the destruction and savage denial of said feeling. This is how the Bible inaugurates the story of man. Rather than a brother to be loved, Abel largely represents a traumatic event for Cain, one that signals the impossibility of his being "everything." The birth of Abel deprives Cain of his privileged position in the affections of his mother; because of Abel, he is no longer Eve's only son. He responds to this defeat by unleashing his violent hatred on his brother. He will tolerate no disruption to his own being. He cannot allow for his standing as the only child to be compromised by the arrival of another. The illusion that prompts his act is, therefore, deeply narcissistic. Cain is defending his privilege and image as the only child—as the firstborn—not just of his parents but of all humanity. Because of that, as Lacan has rightly pointed out and as we shall soon attempt ourselves, we must search for the face of Narcissus behind the mask of Cain. Cain, like Narcissus, is obsessed with being the only one, one of a kind, and with cultivating a grand, ideal image of himself. That makes Abel the intruder who has robbed Cain of his ideal image. Psychoanalysis teaches us that firstborns very often experience the arrival of their sibling not as an occasion for a family to celebrate but as the traumatic expulsion from their privileged status as the only child. It is the origin of what Lacan calls "the intrusion complex": the newborn changes the bond between the first child and their parents, acts as a separating event, and, most importantly, forces the firstborn to give up their status as the phallic object that their mother desires.[19] This fatally triggers an aggressive attitude toward the new arrival which corresponds to a negative experience of exclusion and abandonment.

For the first time, Cain encounters someone who is like him and who enjoys his own privileges yet is also different from him. Is it the balance of brotherhood that primarily generates the conflict? Or is it the imbalance of the children's relationship with their parents? Experience often proves that it is very rare to find blood relations who love one another and share a positive feeling of siblinghood. In addition, Cain is not only the first child of Adam and Eve. He is also—as we already mentioned—the first child of all humanity. Metaphors aside, before the birth of his brother Abel, Cain is *the only living child in the world*. At least in the early stage of his life, Cain achieves the subconscious dream of all children: to be the only one, the most beloved, the one child in the world. What inevitably and tragically shatters Cain's narcissistic image of himself as the absolute One with no Other is Abel's birth. Abel's intrusive birth obligates Cain to experience the trauma of alterity, irreducible difference, and the eruption of the Second (embodied by Abel) onto the scene of the First (Cain as only child). That is why hatred always precedes love when it comes to like and like. The new brother's entrance embodies the trauma of a painful intrusion. In a now famous passage in his *Confessions* referenced by Lacan,

Augustine describes the pangs of jealously felt by a child looking on as his brother suckles at the breast of their mother:

> So the weakness of infant limbs compasses innocence, but with the minds of infants it is not so. I have observed and experienced a little one expressing jealousy. Though he was not yet capable of speech, he glared, pale with envy, at his sibling at the breast.[20]

Cain is overcome with violent urges the moment he feels he has been supplanted by Abel. A third party has driven a wedge between the original mother-son pair. The intrusion of the Other (the trauma of their existence) forces me into a relationship (to compete for love) and disabuses me of the illusion that I ever occupied a central position. Molière's Alceste is filled with the same resentment. His hatred is prompted by his sense that *one can never be* the *one*. That is the origin of envy; the jealous person appears tortured by the life of the Other, by their mere existence. As has been noted, what we really envy is life itself.

Nevertheless, to fully appreciate why Cain murders his brother, we need to look beyond his firstborn narcissism—for Cain was indeed the only child in the world—and examine the nature of Eve's desire for Cain. André Wénin has emphatically pointed out this side of Cain's story, noting the obvious incestuous delirium that haunts Eve's experience of giving birth to Cain.[21] Eve does not just give birth to a son; she gains a man. The Bible puts it eloquently: Eve "became pregnant and gave birth to Cain. She said, 'With the help of the Lord I have gotten a man'" (Gen. 4:1). This is the foundation of the incestuousness

that in Wénin's reading characterizes the primary relationship between Cain and his mother. The Bible says so without hesitation. Eve practically sequesters him: son belongs
to mother, has no life of his own, is captivated by his own
reflection in his mother's gaze. Their relationship lacks the
proper symbolic distance, all is muddled, and there is no
third party, no symbolic mediation represented by the
father. Cain has no life of his own because he is an incestuous son—the exclusive property of his mother. He is
held captive to Eve's desire to get back at his father. Cain
hates Abel as a rival who has broken the spell of their
fusional relationship, the enjoyment of the One fusing
with the Other. Abel is an intruder who stands between
Cain and his mother and breaks up their incestuous relationship. Cain's hatred of his brother is triggered by the
disenchantment of the One that the "extra" child causes.[22]
Yet Cain's first dramatic experience is not the intrusion of
his brother but rather his abduction by his mother, which
brands Cain a passive object of his mother's desire more
than an individual. This branding triggers a narcissistic
fantasy in him: Cain wants to be the sole son in the world,
the only one to fill the void in Eve. In psychoanalytical
terms, his existence appears arrested, entirely identified
with the imaginary phallus of his mother. Just as
Sophocles' Oedipus, in Freud's reading, murders his
father to remain close to his mother, to become her hus-
band and the father of his children/siblings, Cain murders
Abel to remain close to Eve, to continue to be the one
"man" in her life. Both Oedipus and Cain are children
who cannot detach themselves from their origins or imag-
ine themselves as rightful heirs. They will not tolerate los-
ing a pleasure that excludes lack, nor do they consent to

the incision performed by the Law of language. Oedipus and Cain are equally incestuous. Where Oedipus marries his mother Jocasta and fathers children with her (children who are also his siblings), Cain supplants Adam as the man in Eve's life. It is expropriation by way of appropriation: Cain and Eve's incestuous relationship expropriates the father and unites mother and son, and vice versa. So, as the Bible makes clear, Cain becomes his mother's man.

The traumatically intrusive birth of Abel can only be understood in the context of this fusional bond between Cain and his mother. It is not a twinship phenomenon, as it is with Esau and Jacob, but the intrusion of the second child, Abel, an intrusion on Cain's life and, more importantly, on Cain's life with Eve. Abel finds himself paradoxically placed in the symbolic position of the father who winds up dispossessing Cain of his status as the son/imaginary phallus and barring him from maternal enjoyment.

We often encounter this kind of situation in clinical practice. Freud describes a patient who found himself in a similar situation. The birth of the patient's sibling caused a traumatic rupture in his life. Freud proposes the following reconstruction for his patient:

> Up to your nth year you regarded yourself as the sole and unlimited possessor of your mother; then came another baby and brought you grave disillusionment. Your mother left you for some time, and even after her reappearance she was never again devoted to you exclusively. Your feelings towards your mother became ambivalent, your father gained a new importance for you . . .[23]

God's Choice

Enviers never merely envy that which belongs to those they envy, but, as stated earlier, envy the very life of the envied, which appears to them more vibrant than their own. Did Cain strike his brother because he saw him as embodying "more life"? If we follow the letter of the Bible, shouldn't we enlarge the scope of our study to take into account God's role in the brothers' relationship? If Cain sees his brother as an intruder who has usurped his phallic-narcissistic status, it is because God, not Eve, favors Abel.

The scene is well known. When the two brothers make offerings to the Lord, the Lord happily accepts Abel's and rejects Cain's. This rejection opens the narcissistic wound that will trigger Cain's act. It is not until after the Lord has shown that he prefers Abel's gifts to his own that Cain raises his hand against Abel.

We frequently find that human acts of violence are caused by experiences of non-recognition. A failed effort to be recognized—being rejected—is often the source of human violence. It can easily erupt when one is not heard, accepted, or recognized. If the dialectic of recognition is obstructed, blocked, or distorted, violence is one possible outcome. Is that the case with Cain? Has his appeal for recognition and love, implied by the gifts he offers to God, been humiliated by God's refusal? Isn't it this refusal which irritates, burns, and provokes in him deep resentment? Cain feels judged by the Other when he stands before God; he can no longer boast of being his mother's man, the phallic fulfillment she can't live without, her only son. He encounters a Law, in the form of God's judgment, that separates him from his incestuous fusion with his mother.

This is a crucial part of the biblical tale. God rejects Cain's gifts and embraces Abel's. What accounts for his preference is not clear. His judgment remains a mystery. All we know is that Abel's gifts come from sheep farming and Cain's from working the land. Abel is a man in motion and Cain is rooted to the earth. Does Cain's entrenchment further reflect his incestuous dependency on his mother (Mother Earth)? Is that why God rebuffs him? Is Cain too attached to Mother Earth to offer something genuinely his own? This suspicion can be traced to the very name Cain. "Cain" derives from the Hebrew word *qaneh*, meaning "to possess," "to acquire." Hence Cain is "he who was acquired," "he who was possessed." Does the mark of incest diminish his individuality then? Is that why God prefers Abel's gifts?

One thing is certain: the existence of Cain is poorly knit to the place of the Other. The initial violence of incestuous abduction precedes and makes possible his fratricidal act. Looking at Cain's gifts, God drastically upsets the maternal logic of which child is privileged. Therefore, his judgment represents the paternal trauma that Cain suffers. God forces him to see that he is not the only child, not the one and only. If, in the affections of a mother, every child is genuinely *unparalleled*, it follows that no child can feel *unparalleled*.[24]

Gazing at Abel and his offerings, God acts as a separating agent. As Wénin rightly suggests, "the presence of Abel forces Cain to mourn his exclusivity, his fusion, his totality."[25] Confronted with the trauma of this symbolic castration, Cain appears "downcast" and "angered" (Gen. 4:6). His countenance isn't lost on God, who addresses him paternally and tries to soothe his narcissistic wound. Hold your head up, God tells him, envying the Other will poison your life and inevitably lead you to sin. But Cain will not listen to reason, and his anger is prelude to the murder. Nevertheless, in his address to Cain God insists on acting as a father, on not letting Cain fall prey to envy, on offering him the chance to interpret the symbolic meaning of the ill will that has overcome him. *Not being the only son* does not mean that one is worthless, *does not mean one isn't unique*. On the contrary, God urges Cain to hold his head up, to "do what is right" (Gen. 4:7) and to see the Law of castration as a creative opportunity and not merely a disappointment.

Cain finds himself in the same spot as his parents when they were forbidden from eating from the tree of knowledge. And like his parents, instead of embracing the Law of castration as an opportunity to subjectivize his desires, he remains filled with envy. He still appears downcast, his anger is still evident. Cain is unable to submit to the experience of the impossible, to view the Law as liberating him from his incestuous bond rather than depriving him of his desires, to forgo the spoils of being the only child and become a man. In his eyes—as in the eyes of the serpent in the earthly garden—God has committed a grave injustice by preferring Abel's gifts to his own. To him, God's choice is an abusive whim, the act of a despot. But in reality Cain does not tolerate the existence of the Other—his alterity—which God's choice is meant to evoke and make palpable. Rather than look upon God's act as a chance for personal growth, Cain remains a prisoner to narcissism and fixates on reclaiming his absolute rights.

The Lord reads Cain's gloomy withdrawal as a premonition of his desperate act. But God can do nothing but respect the free will of his creature. After listening to God, Cain speaks to Abel. The Bible does not linger over their discussion or go into detail about what it is the brothers discuss. All we know is that Cain turns to speak to his brother. What did he expect would happen? What did he say to Abel? What words did he utter? The Bible keeps mum about their conversation. All we know is that, if they did speak, whatever was said was not enough to assuage Cain's jealous hatred. The Law of the word is interrupted and replaced with the lawlessness of fratricide. It is a familiar lesson. When dialogue ends, when words fail, violence erupts. It is the exact opposite of the process of humanization, which is characterized by renouncing violence and being open to talk.

Cain's act also lays bare the connection between violence and depression. If a human being does not keep their "head high," if they are "downcast" or consumed by jealousy and anger, they risk acting out of desperation, doing evil rather than good, and ceding to death rather than producing life. Goodness, as God reminds Cain before he commits murder, is reserved for those who do not let themselves get defeated, who do not let life irritate them, who do not turn their back on life.

The Fascination of Hatred

Cain does not tolerate God's choice. He does not tolerate God's having refused his gifts and preferred Abel's. He does not tolerate his brother's life, which appears to him more vibrant and better acknowledged than his own. He does not tolerate no longer being the only son. This is how the Bible broaches the important theme of brotherhood and parentage, with Cain's first, traumatic failure. The origins of violence and the human struggle to build a brotherly relationship are one and the same. Cain's act is an attempt to sever that relationship and defend his being the One as opposed to the Other. So, if we want to ponder the problem of brotherhood with any seriousness, we must never forget the perverse connection between Cain's destiny and the (suicidal) destiny of Narcissus. At bottom, the source of jealous hatred is self-love, love of one's own identity, love of one's own "I."

The Bible does not use Cain to interrogate the social origins of violence. Instead, it attempts to penetrate the innermost workings of the psychic origins of violence. Cain's act is a reaction not to oppression but to *fascination*. This is what leads Lacan to propose we read Cain via the figure of Narcissus. Like Narcissus, Cain is not, in fact, able to face alterity, to put up with the reality of twoness, the thorny reality of relation.

What is the object of Cain's envy? Why does he strike his brother dead? We have seen why: the Father appears to love his brother more. Cain, on the other hand, is held hostage to his mother's incestuous desire. Abel embodies what Cain would like to be but cannot be. Those who experience jealousy love their "I" more than life itself; therefore, the presence of another "I" casting a shadow over their image is intolerable. This is the connection between Cain's act and the suicidal passion of Narcissus. According to Lacan's theory, Cain murders Abel with the intent of destroying the seat of his irreversible alienation.[26] His brother incarnates the duplication or scission of the One, the trauma of "relation" that expels One from the incestuous bubble, and it is on account of that duress that Cain seeks to destroy him. Cain's hatred is not ideological. It does not spring from mere privation. Nor is it governed by frustration but by the wound to Cain's ego caused by Abel's presence in the world. In this way Cain's actions closely resemble those of Narcissus. The myth of Narcissus reveals the extremely destructive human tendency to be held captive by our own "I." Ovid tells the myth and Freud retells it: reaching out to his ideal image, and rejecting an encounter with otherness, Narcissus ends up drowning as he attempts to become one with his reflection in the pool of water. His passion is suicidal because it does not recognize the experience of the impossible; he blindly longs for coincidence and totality. That is why, according to Lacan, the myth of Narcissus lays the foundation for human violence in general.

This idea accepts the theory of the "mirror stage," which explains the primary genesis of the "I." A child who is not yet conscious of their individuality, between the age of six and eighteen months, observes in the mirror their ideal image without, however, being able to grasp or coincide with it. That condition—of vulnerability, physical helplessness, and vital dependency—causes the infant to feel fragmented on the other side of the virtual self in the mirror. The image of the self that the child sees reflected in the mirror appears as ideal as it is unattainable. While the real infant inhabits a fragmented body (*corps morcelé*), the mirror reflects back a monumental, statuesque, idealized version of the self. Seeing their own image in the mirror helps children connect their bodies to an ideal image and recognize themselves as subjects endowed with an identity, at the cost, however, of a tragic and irreversible disorientation. No human being can ever coincide with their ideal "I" reflected in the mirror. Instead, the image alienates the subject, given that the reflection is as grandiose as it is unattainable and cannot coincide with the subject's real being. While on the one hand the mirror allows the child to grasp their actual identity because it differs from the image reflected back to them, on the other hand that reflection bars them from ever coinciding with such an image.[27] Our life would be nothing, then, but a vain attempt to make our real being coincide with its narcissistic-ideal representation. So Narcissus' drama becomes crucial to fully understanding the drama of Cain. The brother killer finds in Abel the ideal image that he would like to be but cannot be, making Abel the seat of his alienation. Indeed, Abel is both an ideal object and a rival. Like Narcissus, Cain can't cope with the fact that he is unable to coincide with the ideal image of himself that the mirror has irreversibly stolen from him. Therefore, he strikes Abel with the same criminal ferocity that men alone, and not animals, are capable of. Yet as God reminds him, by lashing out at his brother Cain is only lashing out at himself. The existence of Abel reveals Cain's painful incompleteness; like Narcissus, he is unable to experience alterity, Twoness, the unavoidable intrusion of "relation."

As we have already seen, entering into "relation" with the Other is initially obstructed because Cain has been sequestered by his mother. Like Oedipus, he is swept up in an intense and fatal symbiosis with his mother. He hates alterity for traumatizing the incestuous bond he has formed with her. His deadly confrontation with Abel must be viewed in this context. Abel is the externalized ideal of Cain; God's preference for Abel's gifts over Cain's own makes the image of Abel even more ideal and unattainable. Cain experiences a drama of *self-fascination* that leads him to cancel out the existence of Abel for wounding his ego. Only by murdering his ideal brother can he try to narrow the gap between his self and his image in the mirror; by lashing out at Abel, Cain lashes out at his own unattainable ideal self.

The story of Cain teaches us a profound lesson about the origins of human violence, one that anticipates some theories of psychoanalysis. Violence is not, as Wénin's commentary on Cain seems to suggest, a simple matter of humans regressing to an animal state.[28] Rather, violence dramatically underscores man's dependency on narcissism, his fatal fascination with his own ideal image, his difficulty accepting otherness, the suicidal calling of self-love. Human violence arises not from a regression to an animal state but from a *topical regression to the narcissistic illusions of the mirror*. Hence, in every hardened persecutor, we can easily find an unconscious continuity with the (permanent and indestructible) object of his hatred. In the face of the envied victim, we can spy the ideal image of the person who took their life.

Psychoanalysis defines "projection" as a defensive process during which we attribute to others those obscure parts of ourselves that we cannot integrate into our normal personality. What yokes us to our enemies is radical, disturbing ambivalence. The xenophobe, the fascist, the intolerant—that is the person closest to us, the person who lives inside us prior to being embodied by another. That means that my greatest enemy is always the one who prevents the world from taking on my own image, since his existence is to blame for depriving me of that possibility, for making it impossible for the world to coincide with my image.

BROTHERHOOD, MOURNING, AND RESPONSIBILITY

C ain's act reveals that brotherhood—and, for that matter, parenthood—is never a bond based on blood. His tale shows us that the first brotherly relationship on Earth ends in murder. Have we repressed this origin of every sibling relationship, then?

The Bible is pointing to a fundamental truth here: there is no such thing as biological or natural brotherhood. Meaning there is no such thing as brotherhood without acknowledging that we are ethically responsible for our siblings. After murdering Abel, Cain is asked by the Lord point-blank: "Where is Abel, your brother?" (Gen. 4:9). His appeal is direct. The Lord knows what happened to Abel, but he questions Cain because he wants to hear him say it, to test his sense of ethical responsibility. Once again he turns and addresses him. This time with a question. Where is Abel, your brother? The Lord fills the scene of the crime, the place where the Law of the Word was interrupted, with the word. The brother killer responds testily, refusing to enter into dialogue or admit his guilt. "I don't know," he replies. "Am I my brother's keeper?" (Gen. 4:9). As Wénin has pointed out, God asks the same question of Eve when she commits the first sin: "What is this you have done?" (Gen. 3:13).[29]

In the first episode, God demands an explanation for

the crime. In the second, the word of God takes the side of the slain brother: "What have you done? Listen! Your brother's blood cries out to me from the ground" (Gen. 4:10). The voice of God translates the voice of the murdered brother's blood. Abel's blood speaks. Then God curses Cain just as he had the serpent: "Now you are under a curse and driven from the ground, which opened its mouth to receive your brother's blood from your hand" (Gen. 4:11). But Cain plays down the gravity of his unforgivable act, at least at first, declining to accept responsibility for his brother. By not accepting responsibility Cain shows no sense of fraternal feeling. Our natural assumptions of brotherhood are turned upside down when Cain can only acquire the name "brother" after he has committed his crime and admitted his unforgivable guilt, which is to say only after the subjectification of responsibility for his act.

It is not, therefore, the act of murder that destroys brotherhood. If anything, in the biblical story, murdering one's own brother, and the guilt that murder occasions, actually inspires fraternal feeling. In other words, one has to pass through a stage of *mourning one's kin* in order to construct a sense of brotherhood with those who are not our actual kin, who are not blood, who are strangers to us. That is the ethical responsibility that God seeks to steer Cain toward; to introduce a concept of brotherhood that is stripped of the illusions of country and blood. Which is why human communities always originate from deadly acts. Cities are built over the blood of brothers—as, for example, with Romulus and Remus prior to the foundation of Rome. Abel leaves behind no children; only Cain produces a line. Yet God has first to be severe with Cain:

"When you work the ground, it will no longer yield its crops for you. You will be a restless wanderer on the earth" (Gen. 4:12). God's curse forces Cain out, into history, cutting his incestuous ties to his mother and his homeland. The land that had always rewarded his labors handsomely is destined to turn barren, to cease to yield fruit.

Violence generates nothing but death, destruction, sterility, and despair. The earth is stained with the blood of the slain brother. Cain's act is anti-generative: rather than expand life, it shrinks it. Earth will no longer be home, country, or mother. It is revealed to be a place of exile. As a result of God's curse, Cain must labor to make the land bear fruit and wander the earth with no place to lay his head. Cain, the murderer, will be "a restless wanderer." Yet his curse is all that enables him to adopt a new demeanor. And he does. His tone changes. Whereas Cain initially chooses to answer God ("Where's Abel, your brother?") with denials and deflection ("Am I my brother's keeper?"), when he next answers God he chooses to take the more tortuous path of assuming responsibility for his actions. Cain recognizes his guilt; he himself describes it as unforgivable: "My crime is greater than what may be forgiven" (Gen. 4:13).[30]

When he describes his guilt as unforgiveable, Cain proves that he is an ethical individual. He does not ask to be pardoned, or play down the horror of his act, or hide. We must neither overlook this acceptance of guilt nor consider it an obvious choice, since, as we saw earlier, prior to this Cain was convinced that he had been unjustly overlooked by the Lord when the Lord expressed favor for Abel. The vengefulness that had sprung from his jealous hatred of his brother has now waned. "My crime is greater than what may be forgiven," he says, recognizing the horrific imbalance between what he felt and what he did. Cain is faced with the terrible truth of his act. As in Sophocles' *Oedipus*, the truth is revealed through the ethical experience of guilt. It is not about responding to a moral judgment but facing the consequences of one's actions. One cannot embark upon an ethical life without assuming responsibility for what one has done. So it is for Oedipus: only by admitting his guilt is he liberated from his fate as a parricide. But this guilt is not just a sad figure of morality. Oedipus' guilt, like Cain's, is an ethical figure that allows the individual to make a fresh start. It is not merely about atoning for a crime, but—because he takes responsibility for his actions—starting over from scratch.

This turn of events leads Cain to humanize his existence, finally separating himself from his blood relations. The end of the symbiotic relationship that tied him to his mother opens the way for his journey in exile. Being ejected from the land, from his own soil, coincides with acquiring a new freedom. Cain is no longer a son; he has become a man. The Bible makes this point clear: "So Cain went out from the Lord's presence and lived in the land of Nod, east of Eden" (Gen. 4:16). His is a separation that can be found in other crucial passages in the Bible, for example Abraham's leaving his homeland or the parable of the prodigal son in the Gospel of Luke.[31]

The Lord intervenes to relieve Cain of his guilt, impeding it from simply presaging his death. Cain gloomily thinks that "whoever finds me will kill me" (Gen. 4:14). His admission of guilt makes him a murderer in people's eyes. The imminent risk is that violence will beget violence in a chaotic, never-ending escalation. Once again, the figure of the mirror reigns: the one who struck his brother with impunity will be struck in turn, the murderer murdered. Only God's intervention breaks the mirror and keeps violence from repeating forever. In God's eyes, Cain's guilt should not only be sanctioned but become an occasion for beginning anew. That is why, once Cain accepts responsibility for his actions, God "marks" him: "Then the Lord put a mark on Cain so that no one who found him would kill him" (Gen. 4:15). The mark is symbolic. It humanizes Cain and forbids anyone from killing him. Thanks to this mark, Cain is no longer associated with murder. The mark recognizes him as a man who has committed a grave error and has acknowledged it is unforgiveable.

Hence the fratricide is elevated to brother status and brotherhood liberated from blood ties and the land, from family lines and primary fusional bonds. The mark that God puts on Cain shields the killer from being killed in a brutally specular repetition compulsion. On the one hand, this sign reminds us of the trauma of fratricide and the brother's death—it is the mark of mourning.[32] On the other, it represents Cain's acquisition of individuality, which finally detaches him from his incestuous upbringing. It paves the way for a new symbolic brotherhood, one not founded on narcissistic envy or family lines, or on country and blood, but on a shared sense of ethical responsibility toward one's neighbor and unknown brother.

God wanted to put an end to the deceptions of brotherhood founded on narcissistic envy and the illusion of blood and nature. That is why God does not stop at penalizing Cain but acts to protect him from those who would have him dead. In order for there to be a human community, the specular nature of fratricidal violence must be interrupted. By placing a mark on Cain's forehead before leaving him to his fate, God points to the existence of another Law, one that is different from the specular, punitive or "mimetic" law. God, who symbolizes the Law, does not relish exercising the Law. Rather, he interrupts the "moralistic" reflex of the Law to grant individuals another chance; disables the *mimetic system of the Law*, which answers evil with evil in an endless cycle; and ushers in *another version of the Law.*[33] God does not simply require the mimetic punishment of evil with evil, violence with violence. Nor does he require the law be rid of the logic of retaliation.[34] Instead, he prefers releasing Cain from the incestuous prison and deceptions of narcissistic rivalry that afflicted Cain and gave rise to his action.

CAIN'S LEGACY

C ain's rejection of twoness, which culminates in his fratricidal act, is a rejection of the alterity of the Other as well as a rejection of his own individuality, of the otherness and secret that all human beings bear. Abel's death is the death of our bond with the Other. It is also the death of the subject's individual difference. If the Other cannot be reduced to the One, if his alterity pushes back against my identity, then Cain's act is a manifestation of humankind's persistent, iron will to destroy any relationship with the Other. And if Abel is the seat of Cain's alienation, then suppressing Abel sustains the illusion that the One can ultimately be reconstructed and pacified, that there can be a return to the "One-all-alone."

Cain's act displays his narcissistic desire to reduce two to one and cancel his relation with the Other. It stands to reason that among Cain's descendants we must count those who built the Tower of Babel. The individual act of Cain and the collective act of the Babylonians are, in fact, bound by a common thread. Both reject the inescapable nature of relation, difference, and the insuppressible alterity of twoness. In this sense, the biblical story of Babel is really a continuation of Cain's story. We must read them as the most disquieting and profound legacy of the son who killed his brother. The Babylonians, like their progenitor, strive to build a human community that excludes difference. They want to erect a city that suppresses the plurality of languages and races, a closed city made up of "one people" who speak "the same language" (Gen. 11:6).

No wonder, then, that every radical form of violence and racism springs from the idea that Truth is the incontrovertible site of the One.[35] Indeed, all forms of fundamentalism believe they possess the Truth, as if the Truth were a Thing. Such an illusion inspires the passionate ideology that Hannah Arendt has provided us a profile of—a profile that, in many respects, remains unequaled.[36] Cain's violence rears its head again in the irrational and racist plan that animates the men of Babel: to erase difference, unify languages, and give rise to one people. Babylonian fundamentalism descends directly from Cain's desperate narcissism. At least Cain, in his desperation, can acknowledge his guilt, which action serves as a corrective for having killed his brother. As he labors and wanders the earth, Cain can continue on his way without fear that his crime will come back to haunt him. It is a kind of slow rebirth. The same happens in the flood when it is only through death that the world can be reborn and God commit to stop cursing the earth—which unleashed the flood—and destroying his creation: "Never again will I curse the ground because of humans" (Gen. 8:21). Is that not the same variation on the Law that we witnessed at the conclusion of Cain's story?

Although humans might still prove corrupt, might continue to lead dissolute and sinful lives ("every inclination of the human heart is evil from childhood," Gen. 8:21), God himself becomes aware that wiping everything out and starting over again from scratch is an expression not of the will to live but of the will to die.[37]

Cain's story does not end with God's curse or with his becoming a "restless wanderer." The Bible divorces Cain from being identified with a Manichaean version of evil by making him the first person capable of building a city. This is an important epilogue to his tormented story: if humans can accept the consequences of their actions, their lives will be ethically generative. Not only can good come from good; good can come from evil, too.

That is the message Cain bears. Once God has condemned him to a life of wandering, albeit after protecting him with a mark, Cain's first actions are no longer motivated by the narcissistic fury of jealous hatred but instead appear to be doubly generative. He becomes a father and, at the same time, "the builder" of the first city in human history (Gen. 4:17). Jealous hatred, which seeks to cancel out all forms of alterity, gives way to the symbolic work of rebuilding the Other with the individual birth of his son and the collective birth of a city. It is not by chance that son and city are given the same name—Enoch—which in Hebrew means "inaugurated, dedicated." This twofold creation underscores the fact that Cain's errancy does not impede him from proving capable of desire. Cain's original fundamentalist plan—to destroy the Other as the seat of his alienation—is here subverted; the plurality symbolized by the life of son and city marks a break from the narcissistic identity of the One.

In this second stage, Cain subjectivizes his guilt, makes up for his past by being ethically responsible, which enables him to build without first destroying, to recognize that being in relation—with son and city—is the most authentic form of brotherhood. His vengeful urge is supplanted by an urge to build. So, he reconstructs a new version of brotherhood, one free of the deadly seduction of the mirror and the natural illusion of blood and country.

In fact, brotherhood is an emblem of the insurmountable, binding nature of being in relation with the Other, not with one's blood brother or next of kin so much as with those we do not know, with the brother who has as yet no name.

Notes

With one exception (see note 30) all quotations from the Bible are taken from the *New International Version* (1978).

[1] Sartre's "atheism" defines human desire as a "*désir d'être Dieu*"("a desire to be God"). This desire would deny that one is not God in order to achieve a totalization of being, which in reality is always unattainable. Cf. Sartre, Jean-Paul. *Being and Nothingness: A Phenomenological Essay on Ontology.* Translated by Hazel E. Barnes. Washington Square Press, 1992.

[2] Deleuze, Gilles. "Coldness and Cruelty." *Masochism.* Translated by Jean McNeil. Zone Books, 1991.

[3] Freud, Sigmund. "Our Attitude Towards Death." *Thoughts for the Times on War and Death.* Translated by James Strachey. Hogarth Press, 1957.

[4] Ibid. *Civilization and Its Discontents.* Translated by Joan Riviere. Hogarth Press, 1973.

[5] Ibid. "Our Attitude Towards Death."

[6] Levinas, Emmanuel. *Totality and Infinity: An Essay on Exteriority.* Translated by Alphonso Lingis. Duquesne University Press, 1969.

[7] For more on this subject, in particular the dependent-independent relationship between the created and Creator, see Silvano Petrosino's *La Prova della libertà* (San

Paolo, 2013) and *Emmanuel Levinas* (Feltrinelli, 2017), pp. 22-34, 99-104.

[8] Cf. Hegel, G.W.F. *Early Theological Writings*. Translated by T.M. Knox and Richard Kroner. University of Pennsylvania Press, 1971.

[9] Sequeri, Pierangeli. *Il timore di Dio*. Vita e Pensiero, 2010, p. 52.

[10] The author Ernst Bloch reimagined the serpent as a revolutionary who goads man into freeing himself from the cruel tyranny of God. Like the serpent, Bloch views God's behavior toward his creatures as reflective of an unscrupulous and unpitying tyrant. Only the capriciousness of an omnipotent sovereign, he argues, could create a despotic Law applied to humans but not himself. Cf. Bloch, Ernst. *Atheism in Christianity: The Religion of the Exodus and the Kingdom*. Translated by J.T. Swann. Verso Books, 2009.

[11] Cf. Lacan, Jacques. *The Seminar of Jacques Lacan XVIII: On a Discourse that Might not Be a Semblance*. Translated by Cormac Gallagher. Lacan in Ireland, 1971, www.lacaninireland.com. On various occasions, I have written about the idea of "deadly enjoyment," including from a clinical perspective. See, for example, Recalcati, Massimo. *Jacques Lacan. Desiderio, godimento e soggetivazione*. Raffaello Cortina, 2012, vol. I, pp. 494-496.

[12] Sequeri, Pierangeli. *Il timore di Dio*. Vita e Pensiero, 2010, pp. 57-58.

[13] Cf. Saint Ambrose. "Cain and Abel" in *Hexameron, Paradise, Cain and Abel*. Translated by John J. Savage. The Catholic University of American Press, 2003.

[14] Cf. Freud, Sigmund. "Instincts and their Vicissitudes" in *Complete Psychological Works of Sigmund Freud, Vol. 14*. Translated by James Strachey. Vintage Classics, 2001.

¹⁵ Cf. Saramago, José. *Cain*. Translated by Margaret Jull Costa. Harvill Secker, 2011; and Camilleri, Andrea. *Autodifesa di Caino*. Sellerio, 2019. For a more nuanced literary take on Cain as a man who, by his action, molds the world after admitting his guilt for the murder of his brother—a murder triggered by his feeling that God loved his brother more than himself—and living in extreme solitude as an exile, see also Mariangela Gualtieri's *Caino* (Einaudi, 2011). For an accurate, if streamlined, reconstruction of classic and modern readings of Cain, see Davide Assael's *La fratellanza nella tradizione biblica. II. Caino e Abele*. Edizioni Fondazione Centro Studi Campostrini, 2017, pp. 37-88.

¹⁶ Cf. Lacan, Jacques. *The Ethics of Psychoanalysis 1959-60: The Seminar of Jacques Lacan, Book VII*. Translated by Dennis Porter. Norton, 1997.

¹⁷ Cf. Freud, Sigmund. "Instincts and their Vicissitudes."

¹⁸ Wénin, André. *D'Adam à Abraham ou les errances de l'humain: Lecture de Genèse 1:1-12:4*. CERF Edition, 2007.

¹⁹ Cf. Lacan, Jacques. *Family Complexes in the Formation of the Individual*. Translated by Cormac Gallagher. Lacan in Ireland, 1938, www.lacaninireland.com.

²⁰ Augustine. *Confessions, Volume I: Books 1-8*. Translated by Cathryn J. B. Hammond. Loeb Classical Library, 2014.

²¹ Wénin, André. *D'Adam à Abraham*; cf. Ibid. "*De la violence à l'alliance. Un chemin éthique inspiré des Écritures*" in *Le Supplément* no. 213. Édition spéciale: Enjeux des morales fondamentales, June 2000.

²² Cf. Bianchi, Enzo. *Adamo dove sei?* Edizioni Qiqajon, 2007, p. 231.

²³ Freud, Sigmund. "Constructions in Analysis" in *The*

Standard Edition of the Complete Psychological Works of Sigmund Freud. Translated by James Strachey. Hogarth Press, 1964.

[24] If I may be so bold, I direct you to my own book on this subject: *The Mother's Hands: Desire, Fantasy and the Inheritance of the Maternal.* Translated by Alice Kilgariff. Polity Press, 2019.

[25] Wénin, André. *D'Adam à Abraham.*

[26] Cf. Lacan, Jacques. *The Seminar of Jacques Lacan: Book 1, Freud's Papers on Technique, 1953-54.* Translated by John Forrester. Norton, 2013.

[27] Cf. Ibid. "The Mirror Stage as Formative of the Function of the I" (1949) in *Écrits: The First Complete Edition in English.* Translated by Bruce Fink. Norton, 2006.

[28] Wénin says of Cain's act: "The blood he spills is a sign that the animal in him has prevailed." Wénin. "*De la violence à l'alliance.*"

[29] Cf. Ibid. *D'Adam à Abraham.*

[30] This is how the verse appears in the Aramaic Bible in Plain English and in the Italian translation quoted by the author. However, it is frequently translated in English as "But Cain answered the Lord, 'My punishment is greater than I can bear!'" [Translator's Note]

[31] For one reading of this parable, see my book, *The Son's Secret: From Oedipus to the Prodigal Son.* Translated by Alice Kilgariff. Polity, 2020.

[32] Cf. Wolf, Edith. "*Les figures de l'ambiguïté*" in *Caïn.* Edited by Jacques Hassoun. Autrement, 1997, p. 44.

[33] This will become one of the central themes of all Jesus' teachings; cf. Recalcati, Massimo. *Contro il sacrificio. Al di là del fantasma sacrificale.* Raffaello Cortina, 2018.

[34] For greater insight into Biblical Law and its function

beyond the punitive/mimetic-retaliatory, see Mazzucato, Claudia. *Dalla parte di Caino. Per una giustizia riparativa.* Verdello, 2018.

[35] According to Lacan, racism strikes at the Other's particular mode of jouissance, of enjoyment. On the one hand, this idea connects hatred to a refusal of the Other's existence, to the irreducible discontinuity of twoness. Different skin colors, manners, attitudes toward women or the body, modes of prayer, lifestyles, and diets—these are rejected because they differ from our own. On the other hand, this idea aims to show that the jouissance that "I" rebuff, the form of life that "I" perceive as foreign, strange, and unassimilable, and which "I" do not tolerate, is not outside of myself, alien, or different. Rather it concerns me, involves me, lives inside me. The fascist, the bigot, and the fundamentalist are always and above all the personality of our "I." "Leaving this Other to his own mode of *jouissance* . . . would only be possible by not imposing our own on him." Lacan, Jacques. *Television* (1974). Translated by Denis Hollier, et al. Norton, 1990.

[36] The illusion that Truth can be reduced to a Thing to be possessed is what sustains all forms of ideological/fundamentalist violence. Life means nothing, for only the abstract Idea exists. This is the totalitarian nature of every idealism. Being is worthless if it departs from the essence of an Idea. Total disregard for individual life matches the violence of a universal Idea. Life should, in fact, be disregarded when it does not correspond to the Idea. Cf. Arendt, Hannah. *The Origins of Totalitarianism* (1951). Penguin Classics, 2017.

[37] Cf. Lacan, Jacques. *The Ethics of Psychoanalysis 1959-60: The Seminar of Jacques Lacan, Book VII.*